Stretching Your Limits 2

Over 30 Step-by-Step Instructions

for Your Leg Stretcher Flexibility Strap

Stretching Your Limits 2

All rights reserved.

Published by 14 Peaks

Edited and formatted by 14 Peaks

Cover Design by Dunkin's Design

Cover Photo Model: Adam Boreland

Models: Adam Boreland, Avery Hagler, Taylor Sambola

Models can be contacted at info@14-peaks.com

ISBN-13:978-1545295021

ISBN-10:1545295026

Table of Contents

Introduction

Welcome to the wonderful world of stretching. You are about to learn some amazing stretching information that can help you stretch your limits.

Enhance your stretching routine with the use of a leg stretcher to take your performance to the next level. You are going to learn how to use your device and so much more about the world of stretching.

It's a long way to the top, but don't worry… we'll help you get there.

Chapter 1
The Importance of Stretching

Stretching may seem trivial, but it just may be one the things you can do that will help you take your workout, performance or competition to the next level.

If you think stretching is a waste of time... try *not* stretching. Sitting on the sidelines due to an injury is considered by many to be the biggest waste of time ever!

Stretching 101

Before going any further, let's talk about what stretching is and what it isn't. Stretching is the process of positioning the body in a way that elongates and lengthens the area's muscles and the soft tissues too.

Proper stretching is *not* bouncing to see how far you can push your body. It is not putting your muscles and soft tissues in danger of ripping or tearing. Well, you can bounce, but it is not good for your muscles.

Stretching is done as a warm-up and at the end of a workout. At the end of a workout is when static stretching is applied and when you gain the most flexibility. You will warm up with dynamic stretching, which gently gets your body ready for exercise.

Why Stretch?

The next time you see a dog, cat or even a baby who's waking up from a good night's sleep, watch what they do. They stretch. Stretching is an instinct that is built into animals and humans alike. It's your body's natural way of preparing your muscles and joints for the  activity you'll encounter while you're awake.

Sometimes, however, our brain clicks on over to full-throttle and bypasses the stretching warmup gear altogether. Life is busy. We have coffee to make, a shower to take and traffic to fight. Who has time to stretch?

Waking up isn't the only time it's important to stretch. It's imperative to do so before a strenuous workout, performance or game. But again, life is hectic and you may be tempted to jump in and start without stretching. Failure to practice a proper stretching routine can result in injuries. Every athlete and exercise enthusiast knows that life is too short to sit it out on the sidelines.

When it comes to performance, art is the act of skillfully carrying out an action, like dance or gymnastics. Therefore, stretching is an art. Stretching in its true form is a graceful and artistic movement that is done with ease, although it can be challenging.

Stretching improperly can be worse than not stretching at all, but when done correctly, it can be the wind beneath your wings that enables you to reach soaring heights.

Stretching does a multitude of beneficial things for the entire body. Here are just a few of the many benefits:

- **Increases flexibility and range of motion in your joints.** Flexible joints make everyday tasks, like lifting a child or going up a flight of stairs, much easier. You can just imagine the difference it makes where working out is concerned.

- **Improves your blood circulation.** Not only does blood flow pump oxygen and nutrients to fuel your muscles with energy, it also helps to remove byproduct waste from muscles too.

- **Relieves stress.** Stress is a killer, and also gives way to diseases and depression. When you are full of stress and anxiety, it's really hard to focus. It's easy to lose your inspiration and motivation. Stretching helps to calm your mind so you can concentrate on your workout, competition or performance.

- **Promotes posture.** Your body flows and functions better when it's aligned. You'll have less aches and pains.

- **Prevents injuries.** Flexible muscles are much less likely to snap or tear.

- **Improves coordination.** The better your balance and coordination, the better you will perform.

- **Warms up muscles.** Stretching actually makes your muscles heat up. Think of spaghetti noodles that become more flexible as they begin to loosen up in boiling water and you'll get the picture of how warming up helps your muscles.

Chapter 2
The Types of Stretches

Now that you know how important stretching is, here's an introduction to the different types of stretches you can do in order to achieve the desired results.

- **Active:** Active stretching is when you stretch a muscle by relaxing it and using a muscle in opposition to it in order to initiate and achieve the stretch. This stretch is done without the aid of leverage, body weight, gravity, a stretching device or strap. Doing the splits is a form of active stretching.

- **Passive (relaxed):** Passive stretching is attained by using assistance from something or someone else such as gravity, leverage, a strap, another person, a stretching machine or your own body weight. The object of passive stretching is to relax the muscle you are stretching and to rely on the external force to secure your position and keep your body in place. The use of a leg stretcher creates a passive stretch exercise.

- **Ballistic:** Ballistic stretching can be passive or active and is characterized by bouncy, jerky, uncontrolled, forced motions. It is frowned upon by many experts because it can easily lead to injury.

- **Dynamic:** Dynamic stretching is achieved by going through a series of comfortable, yet challenging, ranges of motions. It generally requires a certain amount of coordination and is carried out in a controlled, smooth and deliberate manner, unlike ballistic stretches. These are done with skipping, jumping, swinging and other movements. Jumping jacks are one example of dynamic stretches.

- **Static:** The static stretch is the most widely used. It is done by holding a position that is challenging yet fairly comfortable for anywhere between 10 and 30 seconds at a time. Poses in yoga are good examples of static stretches.

- **Isometric:** Isometric stretching does not involve motion but rather uses resistance through tensing of a muscle or group of muscles to achieve results.

- **PNF:** Also known as proprioceptive neuromuscular facilitation stretches, these are done by stretching and relaxing muscles.

This popular method is commonly used in clinical settings and often employed by athletes as well.

Stretching for Ballet

If you are in ballet, you know that it is one of the most demanding, disciplined forms of dance in existence. As a matter of fact, it is referred to as the "foundation of all forms of dance."

While the majority of people believe that ballet is an art and not a sport, it is extremely difficult, and just as a physically demanding as a sport. However, it is also an elegant and creative expression. Regardless of ballet's classification, it is an activity that requires a lot from your body.

While in the past there have been certain physiques that were favored in ballet, such as being around five foot three inches to five foot eight inches and weighing between 85 and 130 pounds, the strict criteria is becoming more lax. One thing that has not changed, however, is the fact that participating in ballet demands  all you have to give… and then some. In order to attain such requirements, you are going to need to rely on stretching to enable your body to flex and perform as a ballerina.

Stretching in the world of ballet is so important that in 2014 the Centers for Disease Control (CDC) decided to require stretch and flexibility training to be implemented before every classical ballet technique class. Yes, it's *that* important!

The root reason for the requirement is that failure to stretch was resulting in an enormous amount of injuries and even in postural alignment deformities. These conditions posed problems that could potentially last a lifetime. Stretching, however, helps to prevent such catastrophes.

Stretching for Gymnastics

Gymnastics is thought by many to be the most difficult sport in the entire world. If you have ever done gymnastics, you can most likely understand why. Between becoming a living, breathing pretzel and splitting your legs down the middle, your body takes a beating and must remain flexible and graceful while doing so.

Cheerleading entails a lot of gymnastics, so it's right up there in difficulty too.

Both are great to sit on the sidelines and watch because great gymnasts and cheerleaders make the moves look so easy, but they are not by any stretch of the imagination.

Gymnasts typically display strength that is nine times their body weight. A female who participates in the sport is required to be able to average a short distance speed of sixteen plus miles per hour while males must be over twenty mph. Not only that, but they must be able to rotate, spiral, balance, lift and much more. Much pressure is put upon the performance of leg muscles, arm muscles, core muscles, hips and the upper torso. In order to be versatile and work many parts of your body, you are going to have to stretch or you could be seriously injured. There's no cartwheeling around that fact.

Stretching for Other Athletic Fields

You'll be hard-pressed to find a sport or physical activity that does not benefit from stretching. Basketball, football, soccer, water skiing, diving, horseback riding, trekking, rock climbing, kayaking, swimming, hiking, snow skiing, snowshoeing, ice skating and running all require stretching to perform at peak level and to avoid injury. Use of the leg stretcher can assist your body in getting ready for all of these.

Chapter 3
The Science of Stretching

If you have read our first stretch book, *Stretching Your Limits*, you know the science behind stretching. Here's a quick recap. When stretching, muscle fibers and tendons elongate, meaning they actually get longer. Blood flow increases to the area being stretched which means more oxygen is sent to the muscle. Oxygen fuels muscles.

But, believe it or not, it's the nervous system that just may have the biggest impact where stretching is concerned. The nervous system controls how far our bodies stretch without injury. When your brain thinks you are stretching beyond what you should, it fires out warning signals of pain and resistance.

Although this state of resistance is intended to protect the body, tense muscles are vulnerable to injuries. With a regular stretching routine, however, you retrain your brain to send out a "coast is clear" message to your muscles instead of a "mayday" warning. That is when your muscles begin to cooperate with the strain you are placing on them. They then become stronger and more flexible.

Muscles 101

It's important to learn how muscles work since you rely on them so much. Your muscles can take you to high places or… can bring you totally down if they fail you.

What Exactly Is a Muscle, Anyway?

Muscles are made of soft tissues. They work to create motion and force. They consist of a special and unique type of elastic tissue that is much akin to the properties of a rubber band. Within each muscle, there are thousands of small fibers.

Smooth, skeletal, and cardiac are the three types of muscles located within your body.

The Jobs of Muscles

Each muscle has a certain role to fulfill. Some have more than one job. There are cardiac muscles that make up your heart that pump blood out. They also constrict and relax in order to let blood flow in. Smooth muscles are responsible for contracting in order to allow hollow organs to work, such as the gastrointestinal tract, blood vessels and bladder. Skeletal muscles play the part of controlling movements of the body, and can also exert force. Smooth muscles work voluntarily, meaning you control them. Your body's posture, your legs and flexing your arm muscles are good examples of smooth muscles you enable by will.

How Do Muscles Work?

Protein filaments containing actin and myosin are found within muscles. They slide by each other and contract, which changes the shape of the cell. It also causes the length to change as well. After a muscle is formed, it is capable of making force and motion like when you rotate your legs in gymnastics.

Muscle Facts

- Your heart is actually made of muscles.

- Your body contains around 650 muscles.

- The word *muscle* is derived from the Latin word meaning *mouse*.

- It takes 17 muscles to smile and 43 to frown!

Types of Muscle Contractions

Eccentric: When something is moved away from the center, it's considered to be eccentric. Lowering your leg back down from a lift position is an eccentric movement. Eccentric moving makes your muscles longer.

Concentric: When you move something toward the center, it is concentric. Your joints move toward the action as well. Jumping forward is one example of a concentric movement. The amount of force needed in order to perform that action is called torque.

Synergists: Muscles that work along with other muscles in order to perform a job are called synergists.

Stabilizers: When a force comes upon them, these muscles hold things in place.

Antagonists: These muscles co-contract and are often used to balance.

We owe a lot of our achievements to the wonderful work that muscles do.

As you direct your efforts and energies to the muscles you are using and understand how they work, you will no doubt find that your use of them will improve.

Chapter 4

Static Stretching

Static stretching exercises assist your body in becoming more flexible. They are done without the use of bouncing or movement and instead rely on holding a certain stretch position. Static stretching should only be done after you have primed the muscles with blood and that requires dynamic stretching first. Using the ballet band or leg stretcher is static stretching.

Benefits of Static Stretching Exercises

1. Flexibility

Interestingly, when you practice static stretching, your tension receptors become less sensitive, so you relax and your muscles are able to relax as well. This causes your muscles to stretch to a longer length, or elongate.

2. Stress and Tension Reduction

Muscles get tense and stressed and then… they get hurt. Tense muscles are at high risk of suffering tears and strains, so it's important to do static stretching.

3. Muscle Group and Range of Motion Focus

Did you know that static stretching can help you to focus on individual parts of your body that you want to concentrate on for performance? It sure can. As you give attention to specific ranges of motions and muscle groups, you can breathe in deeply to let oxygen flow to the areas.

Cellular respiration and ATP energy play a huge role. When you breathe in oxygen, it travels through your bloodstream and some of it goes to your muscles immediately for use right then. Other oxygen is stored by myoglobin, an amazing compound found in your body that incorporates oxygen to break down glucose (blood sugar).

Glucose fuels your muscles. That process is called ATP. When you breathe deeply while stretching, you refuel your muscles.

How far do I stretch?

A rubber band stretches but is limited in how far it can do so before it breaks. It's the same scenario when it comes to our muscles. The viscoelasticity of your muscles is a key factor in determining how long you should remain holding a stretch. It's a good idea to begin gently so you don't stress the muscles and cause injury or discomfort.

Holding your stretches for 10-60 seconds is recommended, although there are a lot of different opinions on the precise length of time that's best. Ultimately, it is up to you to decide. However, many experts say there is no benefit beyond 60 seconds.

How far should you stretch your muscles? The perfect holding length really depends on a couple of things, like viscoelasticity.

Viscoelasticity is the term that denotes the property of an object that has both viscous (resistant) and elastic qualities. It is limited stretching, of sorts.

Stretching Facts

1. Scar tissue can weaken muscles, so be careful not to overstretch areas affected by it.

2. If your muscles are sore or tired, they are more susceptible to injury, but mild stretching can help relieve some of the soreness.

3. Cold muscles injure quicker and more often. That is why you always use dynamic stretching first.

4. Stay hydrated, because muscles and soft tissues need hydration to stretch and stretch back.

5. The collagen and elastin content of your body play a big part in determining how far you can stretch. They are natural bodily substances that assist the body in stretching.

What Makes for the Best Stretch?

The goal is to stretch your muscles as far as you can without pain. If you do have pain, you have over-stretched, so back out a bit. It is imperative not to stretch too far or for too long.

Examples of Static Stretching

*   The middle or side splits.

- Reaching to touch your toes and holding the pose.

- Pulling your legs to your chest while on your back.

- Leaning forward to touch the floor and holding the pose while sitting.

- Using a ballet stretch band to do any of the above exercises.

It's important to note that static stretching isn't supposed to be difficult. It's not supposed to hurt or be uncomfortable. Instead, it is designed to help your body loosen up and stretch out and also to come back together. The purpose is to impart flexibility and to minimize the chance of injury.

Chapter 5
Dynamic Stretching

Warming your muscles up helps keep muscles limber and loose so they are less likely to get injured. Remember the strand of spaghetti and how brittle it is until you put it in boiling water. After warming up, it becomes soft and pliable. The same is true with your muscles. Dynamic stretching is designed to warm your muscles up so they can become pliable.

Dynamic stretching exercises not only warm your muscles up, they get your blood pumping and loosen up your muscles, ligaments, and even your joints to get them primed for exercise.

When you practice dynamic stretching, you're firing up your performance.

Dynamic Stretching:

- Increases your range of motion.

- Causes your heart to pump and your blood to flow to the muscles.

- Promotes warmth for your muscles, ligaments, and joints.

- Increases oxygen flow to your muscles.

- Gets your nervous system stimulated.

- Prepares your muscles and entire body for upcoming strenuous movements.

- Promotes a smooth and thorough warm-up through flowing movement.

- Assists in preventing injuries.

Dynamic Stretch Examples

- Leg swings

- Shoulder rolls

- Hip rolls

- Neck rolls

- Jumping jacks

- Jumping in place

- Arm rolls

- Side bends with constant movement

More about Dynamic Stretches

Remember that all stretching exercises are either passive or active. Dynamic stretching is active stretching. Static stretching is under the category of passive. Dynamic stretch exercises involve motion but static stretching exercises do not.

Dynamic stretching is not ballistic stretching. Ballistic stretching is just as the name implies: stretching that is unruly. Dynamic stretches are more strategic and controlled. They are performed with a gradual increase in speed and reach. Dynamic stretches warm you up in a gentle and controlled fashion.

When you are doing dynamic stretching, it's important not to push your body. Even though the movements are precise and controlled, it is possible to place too much stress on your muscles, joints, and ligaments. That, of course, defeats the purpose of stretching.

Dancing Dynamics

If you will be dancing, dynamic stretches are optimal to warm your muscles up and to get your blood flowing. Dancing relies on cardiovascular activity; the same is true for cheerleading and gymnastics, so priming the pump is smart.

You will want to concentrate on the poses, muscles, stances, and actions that are required while performing the art or sport you are going to be doing and give focus to the areas of use so you can warm them up properly.

Chapter 6
Myofascial Release

Myofascial release takes place when you gently apply sustained pressure into the myofascial connective tissues. It is often done for the purpose of relieving pain and is very popular in the medical field and also in sports medicine. The dance world employs the use of it as well.

Fascia is located within the connective tissue. It is a soft tissue that offers support to muscles and protects them as well. It keeps them from getting injured, but fascia can become tense or tight, which can result in pain and soreness. Such a tense state can prevent proper blood flow to your muscles, which also means they are not getting properly fueled. That is when it is a good practice to massage it.

Releasing the myofascial is beneficial to:

- Eliminate or ease pain

- Improve circulation

- Improve flexibility

- Restore motion

- Promote good posture

- Enhance strength

- Encourage elongation of muscles

- Protect muscles

- Relieve tension

- Break up scar tissue

Myofascial Release

There are a number of ways myofascial release can be performed. It can be administered with expensive equipment found in sports therapy clinics or in hospitals and can also be administered by yourself with simple tools.

Strenuous sports and activities like dance and gymnastics often present the need for such a treatment due to the strain they place on the body. Overworking or over-exercising can lead to the need as well.

If you want to perform myofascial release on yourself, here are some tips of where to do so:

- The back of your calves

- The back of your ankles

- Your IT band

- The back of your quad and your quads in general

- Your shoulders

- Your back

- Your adductors

- The balls of your feet

Myofascial Release Methods

Foam rollers, tennis balls and Theracane devices work miracles. You can employ the use of trigger point therapy tools too. You will benefit from doing so because you won't be distracted by the pain and discomfort and in addition your muscles will be happier and healthier.

Chapter 7

Optimize Your Workout with a Leg Stretcher

Stretching maximizes your workout so you can get to the top of your game. When you stretch using a leg stretcher, the benefits are magnified even more. With regular use of your leg stretcher, you'll be at your peak performance in no time!

What Is a Leg Stretcher?

A leg stretcher is a device that is used to help you stretch and strengthen your leg and lower back muscles. Generally, it has a bracket to attach to the top of a door frame, a pulley and pull cord and a sling. You simply insert your leg into the sling, then raise and lower it in order to target a particular muscle or muscle group.

In order to optimize your stretching routine, you can use a leg-stretching device that will help you stretch properly and effectively.

Practically anyone can use a leg stretcher. As long as you have enough space to move around a little in and a door, ceiling or wall to attach it to and have no serious physical condition that would put you at risk, it should work great for you.

Some of the people who use a leg stretcher are:

- Ballerinas

- Dancers

- Gymnasts

- Runners

- Martial Artists

- Swimmers

- Ice Skaters

- Sprinters

- Climbers

Yet leg stretching devices aren't just for hard-core athletic people. They also work wonders for anyone wishing to:

- Perform a physical activity.

- Promote good balance.

- Promote good posture.

- Limber up muscles and increase range of motion.

- Loosen up muscles to relieve pain.

- Destress.

- Prevent injuries caused by stiff muscles and tight joints.

What Can a Leg Stretcher Do for Me?

If you want to take your stretching to the next level, a leg stretcher can certainly help you out. Stretching is more comfortable and more productive when using the device. It will help you balance and adds resistance so you can reach your stretching goals easier and faster.

One of the best-kept secrets is that a leg-stretching machine can make you have a better appearance too. The next time you are in a crowd, note the difference in the way people carry themselves and what it says for their overall looks. Those with good posture and great balance just seem to glide around the room with ease and confidence. A good stretching routine can help you achieve that air as well.

Types of Leg Stretchers

Leg stretchers are different from leg-stretching machines although, for the most part, they are used for the same goal: to help you stretch. Machines are larger, heavier and take up much more space. They are usually found in gyms or in homes where there is a designated workout room and generally cost a lot more than a leg stretcher.

Leg stretchers attach to a door, a wall or the ceiling. They are portable, inexpensive and are a cinch to use. They basically accomplish the same thing as the machine does… they maximize your stretching.

There are many different styles of leg stretchers and various levels of cost as well. Be sure to get one that is well made, and check out the quality of any stretcher you are considering. Look for package deals as well. Oftentimes you can get one with extras, like a carry bag or additional features, for the same price.

What Kind of Exercises Can I Do with a Leg Stretcher?

Stretches done with the help of a leg stretcher are considered to be static. There are many variances of stretches that can be done with the device so that you can flex different muscles and muscle groups. You'll find plenty of great stretch exercises in this book and you can add in some of your own customizations if you'd like as well.

Setting Up Your Leg Stretcher

Over-the-Door Type

1. Place the smaller strap over the door.

2. Close the door securely.

3. Place the longer strap through the "D ring" and pull it through.

4. Pull the straps to desired length.

5. Check to be sure the device is firmly in place and all parts are working properly.

6. Secure your foot in the loop and begin your stretches.

Ceiling or Wall

1. Drill a hole in the ceiling or wall.

2. Get a heavy-duty bolt type hook (make sure it is strong enough).

3. Screw the hook in securely.

4. Hook shorter strap with "D ring."

5. Pull longer strap through "D ring."

6. Pull straps to desired length.

7. Check to make sure the device is firmly in place and that all parts of the unit are properly working.

8. Secure your foot in the loop and begin your stretches.

Devices with Cables and Pulleys

Some leg stretchers come with cables or pulleys. Instructions vary but should be included in the packaging. Many actually have video instructions, which make the assembly even easier.

Cautions and Concerns

Here are some pointers that can help keep you safe while stretching:

- Always be sure to check with your physician before starting any exercise regime.

- Don't skimp when purchasing your stretching unit.

- Read the instructions that come with your leg stretcher.

- Never push your body past the first inkling of pain and tightness. Work up gradually.

- If you are sick or injured, take a break from serious stretching.

- Keep hydrated.

- Wear appropriate clothing that won't get tangled up in the device.

- If you suspect that the door, ceiling or wall you have your leg stretcher attached to is becoming weak, have it checked out before using the device any more.

- Be sure to lock the door you are using so no one can open it
  and cause you to get hurt.

Chapter 8
Warming Up

Before we get into the "how to" of the leg stretcher exercises, we will go over the warm-up and cool downs. Warming up is vital to a good performance. Think about it this way: a race car driver never just hops in his car and takes off down the dragstrip. To do so would not optimize performance. The same is true of your performance. You must warm up if you want to win.

You'll boost oxygen to your muscles, increase your heart rate and increase your respiratory rate all at the same time when you warm up. You will reap the benefits.

In addition, you can get focused and prepared for the game or performance ahead. You can use this time to visualize a winning performance.

Types of Warm Ups

The chosen warm-up should mimic the type of activity you are participating in that day. Think of the muscles you will be using, the actions you will be taking, and then look for exercises that utilize those areas. If you are dancing, your warm-up plan will most likely be different from that of a marathon runner. It is a good idea, however, to warm up all muscles, but you can focus on those you will use the most.

Stretching can be static which means without movement, or it can be dynamic with movement. You can stretch simply by spreading your legs to the splits position or you can employ the use of a leg stretcher to bring you into a stretch. A stretch band is also an option, as we've learned.

Warming up increases:

Blood Circulation

Warming up increases blood circulation. The small blood vessels, or capillaries, in your muscles are constricted until you start to exercise them. As you begin to move them, your circulation increases. Then, it expands. Remember that blood transports oxygen to fuel your muscles with energy. Now, are you getting the picture as to the importance of warming up? You are, in essence, fueling your muscles with the power and energy that your performance will depend upon.

Body Temperature

As your blood begins to move and flow, it heats up your body and your muscles literally start to get warmer. When this happens, the hemoglobin in your blood expels more oxygen, which is like fueling up a car for the big race.

In addition to warming up your body temperature, stretching gets your blood flowing and oxygen level pumped up. It also makes your muscles contract and relax more rapidly, increases nerve transmission, and optimizes the metabolism within your muscles.

Prevents Injuries

Although it can be tempting to take the fast track and just jump into the action, it is not wise. Warming up can prevent injuries could that happen during your performance or game. A cold muscle can easily rip or tear, so it's definitely worth the extra time and trouble it takes to warm your muscles up.

Flexibility

Warming up increases flexibility because your muscles literally get heated and are much more able to move. And of course, the more flexible and limber your body is, the less likely it is to get injured. Bend but don't break. That's the goal!

Muscle Viscosity

Warming up decreases muscle viscosity. That means it makes them work better. Located in between the muscle layers is a fluid-filled sac. This sac lubricates your joints and muscles with a substance that is known as synovial fluid. The fluid acts as a buffer to prevent your muscles from reacting too hastily when you work them. It slows the contraction of your muscles down  and regulates the force and speed. Muscle viscosity, in short, is the gauge of how well that regulation is functioning. Decreasing muscle viscosity is vital to good performance.

Stretch to Warm, Stretch to Win

By now you are seeing that stretching and warming up are for winners. Both can make or break your game. So, what is the best routine to adopt? Dynamic stretching prior to your workout or performance and cooling down with static stretches is a great game plan. Let's take a look at what a cool-down actually is.

Chapter 9
The Warm-Ups

Warming up is cool. The reason it's cool is because getting hurt is not. By now, you understand that a couple of stretches on the barre are not going to carry you through your performance. A leg up once or twice won't get you through your track event. It is serious and is worth doing right.

Arm Roll Outs aka Swimmers

Rolling your arms out does some very beneficial things to get your body warmed up. It gets your blood pumping and fuels your muscles.

1. Stand tall with your arms to your side.

2. Bring your arms up the sky

3. Roll forward ten times and then backward ten times, like you are doing front crawl in the pool.

4. Repeat ten times.

Jumping Jacks

Let's get that blood pumping! Jumping jacks are a fantastic way to raise your core temperature, which gets everything moving and warmed up.

1. Stand with your feet close together, arms to your sides.

2. Tighten your abdominal muscles so your pelvis is forward and your lower back is straight.

3. Slightly bend your knees.

4. Now, jump so you land with your feet a bit over shoulder-width apart.

5. At the same time, raise your arms above your head. (You should be on the balls of your feet.)

6. With your knees slightly bent, jump again, as you bring your feet together and your arms back to your sides.

7. Repeat fifteen times.

Neck and Shoulder Roll

Your neck is used widely in many sports and activities. Be sure to warm it up well with an exercise like this one.

1. Stand straight and tall with your feet shoulder-width apart.

2. Slowly tilt your head to the side. Gently pull.

3. Repeat on the other side.

Jogging in Place

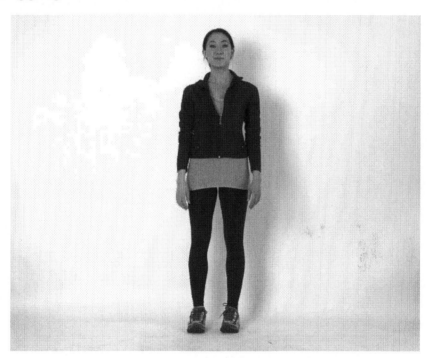

This is a very simple warm-up, but one that is priceless

1. Hold your arms to your side.

2. Breathe deep and slow.

3. Jog gently in place for ten steps on each foot.

4. Gradually pump up the pace ten more steps.

5. Go one more round, even faster.

6. Gradually cool down your pace.

7. Complete with your arms beside you in a stance position.

Rolling It Back and Rolling It Up

This exercise will help your body establish balance and mobility in the neck, back, spine, and hamstrings. It will warm up your abdominal muscles, get your blood circulating, relieve tension, help create space between the vertebrae, and promote proper posture as well.

1. Drop your chin to your chest.

2. Roll through your back reaching your hands to the floor.

3. When you feel the need, bend your knees.

4. Stretch and hold.

5. Slowly, go all the way back up to a standing position.

6. Repeat five to ten times.

Don't stay down and hold it or you turn this into a static stretch. Keep it rolling slowly.

Take Time for the Spine

The health of your spine is crucial, not just in the performing arts and in sports, but for your life in general. The spine is the second most injured body part in dancers, preceded only by leg injuries. It is a leading injury in gymnasts.

Spinal injuries can lead to chronic pain. Here's a warm-up to help make sure your spine is prepared.

1. Kneel on the floor on your hands and knees with your palms directly under your shoulders and your knees under your hip bones. Your fingers will be pointed away from you.

2. Tuck in your chin, and then curve your back upward toward the ceiling. Gently pull.

3. Arch your back, pulling your head up toward the ceiling.

4. Tilt your tailbone up.

5. Return to your original position and repeat five times.

Hip Warm Ups

Warm ups are hip, literally. The hip is another part of the body widely used in ballet, dance, gymnastics, and most any other performing art or sport. You will need a lot of hip flexibility.

Did you know a turnout, the classic ballet starting position with toes and knees turned out and heels together, requires the work of six muscles located deep within your pelvic and hip area?

The hips are often overworked in many of the performing arts and in sports too. Make sure to warm them up each and every time.

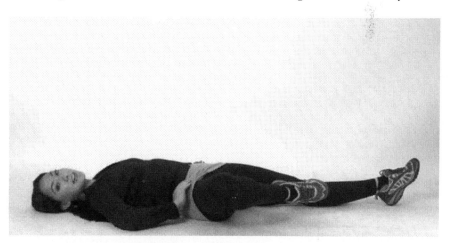

1. Lay down on your back.

2. Pull your right knee to your chest.

3. Circle your bent leg out to the side.

4. Return your leg next to your other leg, lengthwise.

5. Repeat ten times.

6. Switch and do the same using your left leg.

Ankle Rotation Sensation

It goes without saying that your ankles need to be warmed up. Just think of how much weight is put on them solely by walking. It is very important to get them ready to roll or not to roll.

1. Lay on the floor.

2. Gently point the toe of your right foot.

3. Lift your right leg slightly off the floor.

4. Rotate your ankle in a circle.

5. Repeat ten times to the right and ten times to the left.

6. Now, do the same on your left side.

Tip: This exercise can also be done stranding. Sometimes students are asked to write their name with the foot to make it more fun.

Back Legs and Hips Dip

We've talked about how important it is to warm up the hips, but the hamstrings (back of the legs) are super significant too.

1. With your legs wide apart and your feet pointed out, bend your knees.

2. Drop your hips down to the floor to a deep, wide squat.

3. From there, bring one leg out straight to the side as you stretch.

4. Hold for twenty seconds.

5. Do both sides five times.

Chapter 10
The Leg Stretcher Stretches

After warming up you can begin the leg stretcher exercises. If this is your only workout of the day, you can jump right in. If you are going to work out in your sport then this should be done after the workout.

The reason, as stated earlier in the book, is that static stretching is reserved for after the workout, as doing it before the workout can lead to more injuries. There is scientific evidence showing this, but covering that science is beyond the scope of this book

IT BAND KNEE FLEX

Muscles Targeted: IT band, glutes, adductors

1. Stand with your back against the door.

2. Put the strap around your right ankle.

3. Pull down gently until your foot is almost hip level.

4. Hold for 15 seconds.

5. Repeat on the opposite side.

IT BAND KNEE FLEX WITH CALF RAISE

Muscles Targeted: IT band, glutes, adductors, calf of supporting leg

1. Stand with your back against the door.

2. Put the strap around your right ankle.

3. Pull down gently until your foot is almost hip level.

4. Raise your left heel off the ground.

5. Hold for 15 seconds.

6. Repeat on the opposite side.

BACK LEG FLEX PULL

Muscles Targeting: Quadriceps and calves of supporting leg, hamstrings and adductors for lifting leg, hip stability

1. Stand straight and tall, facing sideways.

2. Loop the ankle of your back leg into the leg stretcher.

3. Rotate slowly to where your hip is out externally.

4. Keep your extended leg straight.

5. Pull down gently on the strap with your palms and wrists facing your body.

6. Repeat on other side.

BACK LEG FLEX PULL WITH CALF LIFT

Muscles Targeting: Quadriceps of supporting leg, hamstrings and adductors for lifting leg, hips, calves

1. Stand straight and tall, facing sideways.

2. Loop the ankle of your back leg into the leg stretcher.

3. Rotate slowly to where your hip is out externally.

4. Keep your extended leg straight.

5. Pull down gently on the strap with your palms and wrists facing your body.

6. Raise your heel off the ground and hold for 5 seconds.

BOW STRETCH

Muscles Targeted: quadriceps on supporting leg, back, hips

1. Stand straight and tall, facing sideways.

2. Loop the ankle of your back leg into the leg stretcher.

3. Rotate slowly to where your hip is out externally.

4. Keep your extended leg bent.

5. Pull down gently on the strap with your palms and wrists facing inward.

6. Repeat with the other leg.

BOW STRETCH WITH HEEL RAISE

Muscles Targeted: quadriceps and calf on supporting leg, back, hips

1. Stand straight and tall, facing sideways.

2. Loop the ankle of your back leg into the leg stretcher.

3. Rotate slowly to where your hip is out externally.

4. Keep your extended leg bent.

5. Pull down gently on the strap with your palms and wrists facing inward.

6. Raise your heel off the floor as you exhale by contracting the calves. Hold the top contraction for 15 seconds.

7. Repeat with the other leg.

SIDE LEG PULL

Muscles Targeted: Adductor muscles

1. Stand straight and tall with your back to the door.

2. Put your foot through the loop and then pull your leg out to the side.

3. Pull the strap down gently,

4. Keep your hips aligned and your leg straight.

5. Work the opposite side.

SIDE LEG PULL WITH BALANCE

Muscles Targeted: Adductor muscles

1. Stand straight and tall with your back to the door.

2. Put your foot through the loop and then pull your leg out to the side.

3. Pull the strap down gently and bring the arm above the head as pictured.

4. Keep your hips aligned and your leg straight.

5. Work the opposite side.

SIDE LEG PULL WITH SPLITS

Muscles Targeted: Adductor muscles

1. Stand straight and tall with your back to the door.

2. Put your foot through the loop and then pull your leg out to the side.

3. Pull the strap down gently until you are in a full split. Go very slowly and focus on your balance.

4. Keep your hips aligned and your leg straight.

5. Work the opposite side.

ADVANCED SIDE LEG PULL WITH BALANCE

Muscles Targeted: Adductor muscles

1. Stand straight and tall with your back to the door.

2. Put your foot through the loop and then pull your leg out to the side as you bend at the waist with hips facing forward.

3. Pull the strap down gently, and bring your arm out carefully balancing.

4. Keep your hips aligned and your leg straight.

5. Work the opposite side.

SIDE PULL-CALF RAISE

Muscles Targeted: Adductor of lifting leg, calf of supporting leg

1. Stand straight and tall with your back to the door.

2. Put your foot through the loop and then pull your leg out to the side.

3. Pull the strap down gently

4. Keep your hips aligned and your leg straight.

5. Lift the heel of the foot on the ground up as you pull your other leg up.

6. Work the opposite side.

TOP LEG STRETCH SHOULDERS OUTWARD

 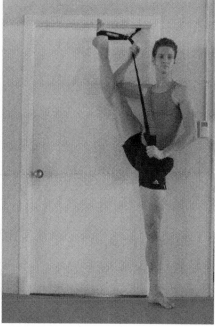

Muscles Targeted: Hamstrings, adductors

1. Stand straight and tall, facing the door.

2. With one foot flat, toes pointing to the door, loop the other foot through the band.

3. Hold the strap with bended elbows, holding it close to your body.

4. Gently pull your leg up with toes pointed.

5. Rotate your shoulders and hips slightly towards your extended leg.

6. Hold for ten seconds.

7. Work the opposite side.

TOP LEG STRETCH SHOULDERS SQUARED

Muscles Targeted: Hamstrings, adductors

1. Stand straight and tall, facing the door.

2. With one foot flat, toes pointing to the door, loop the other foot through the band.

3. Hold the strap with bended elbows, holding it close to your body and hips facing forward.

4. Gently pull your leg up with toes pointed.

5. Hold for ten seconds.

6. Work the opposite side.

CHAIR LIFT

Muscles Targeted: Hamstrings

1. Sit straight up in a chair.

2. Loop one leg through the leg stretcher band.

3. Place the other leg down with pointed toes and leg slightly bent.

4. Slowly and gently pull your leg up.

5. Hold for ten seconds

6. Repeat on the other side.

UP AGAINST THE WALL

Muscles Targeted: Adductors

1. Stand straight with your face to the wall.

2. Loop one ankle into the strap.

3. Plant one foot on the floor, angled outward.

4. Slowly pull the strap to extend your opposite leg up.

5. Hold for ten seconds.

6. Repeat on opposite side.

FRONT LEG PULL

Muscles Targeted: Hamstrings

1. Stand straight and tall, facing the door.

2. With one foot flat, toes pointing to the door, loop the other foot through the band.

3. Hold the strap with bended elbows, holding it close to your body.

4. Gently pull your leg up with toes pointed.

5. Hold for ten seconds.

6. Work the opposite side.

FRONT LEG PULL INTO SPLITS

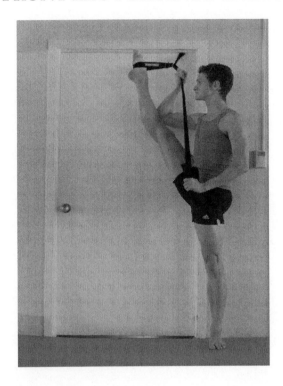

Muscles Targeted: Hamstrings

1. Stand straight and tall.

2. With one foot flat, loop the other foot through the band.

3. Hold the strap close to your body.

4. Gently pull your leg up with toes pointed.

5. Pull until you reach your full extension.

6. Hold for ten seconds.

7. Work the opposite side.

FRONT LEG PULL WITH CALF STRETCH

Muscles Targeted: Hamstrings, calf

1. Stand straight and tall.

2. With one foot flat, loop the other foot through the band.

3. Hold the strap close to your body.

4. Gently pull your leg up with toes pointed.

5. Raise the supporting heel off the ground.

6. Hold for ten seconds.

7. Repeat on opposite side

GET BACK JACK

Muscles Targeted: Adductors, hamstrings, quadriceps

1. Stand facing the side.

2. Plant one foot on the ground, toes facing forward.

3. Loop the band through your other foot with toes pointed.

4. With both hands, gently pull your leg up.

5. Hold for ten seconds.

6. Work the other side.

GET BACK JACK WITH HEEL RAISE

Muscles Targeted: Adductors, hamstrings, quadriceps, calf

1. Stand facing the side.

2. Plant one foot on the ground, toes facing forward.

3. Loop the band through your other foot with toes pointed.

4. With both hands, gently pull your leg up.

5. Raise the supporting calf off the ground.

6. Hold for ten seconds.

CALF STRETCH

Muscles Targeted: Hamstrings

1. From the side hamstring stretch position place your foot in the center of the flexibility strap as shown above.

2. Gently pull your body towards your knee.

3. Hold the pose for twenty to thirty seconds while concentrating on your breathing and the muscles you are stretching.

4. Relax for a few seconds.

5. Switch and repeat on the opposite side.

KNEELING QUADRICEPS STRETCH

Muscles Targeted: Quadriceps

1. Stand with your legs hip-width apart.

2. Loop the band around the middle of your left foot, and then bring it over your right shoulder.

3. Step forward with your right leg and plant your left knee on the floor so it is bent and your right foot is on the ground.

4. With your left hand on the floor, lower your body to where your front left thigh is parallel to the floor. At this point, the flexibility strap should be snug.

5. Hold for twenty to thirty seconds while concentrating on your breathing and the muscles you are stretching.

6. Relax.

7. Switch and repeat on the opposite side.

STANDING FRONT LEG STRETCH

Muscles Targeted: Inner and outer thighs

1. Stand facing a chair.

2. Hold the band with your right hand, wrapping it around your wrist once.

3. Take the other end of the band over your right shoulder and loop it around your left foot.

4. Hold onto the chair with your left hand.

5. Lean forward toward the chair, slightly arching your back.

6. As you are leaning in, bring your left foot up over your head so you are basically doing the splits in the air.

7. Slowly lower your left foot back to the ground while bringing your torso back to a standing position.

8. Hold for twenty to thirty seconds while concentrating on your breathing and the muscles you are stretching.

9. Repeat on the other side.

STANDING QUADRICEPS STRETCH

Muscles Targeted: Quadriceps

1. The next stretch can be done using a wall, a chair, or anything stable. Loop the flexibility strap around the top of your right foot then over your right shoulder and hold it in your left hand.

2. Bend your right leg up at the knee and slightly apply tension to the strap. With your left leg straight and planted on the ground, rest your right hand on the wall.

3. Turn your neck to the left so it stretches slightly.

4. Hold the pose for twenty to thirty seconds while concentrating on your breathing and the muscles you are stretching.

BALANCING STANDING QUADRICEPS STRETCH

Muscles Targeted: Quadriceps, balance

1. Get into the standing quadriceps stretch.

2. Push off the wall.

3. Hold for twenty second. Relax and concentrate on the muscles you are stretching.

4. Repeat for the opposite side.

LEG PRESS FROM GROUND

Muscles Targeted: Lower Back, Hamstring

1. Lie flat on the floor with the middle of the band behind your back at the arch and the ends looped twice around your left foot. Your right leg should be straight.

2. Push your left leg up and hold on to the band with one hand on each side.

3. Hold the pose for twenty to thirty seconds while concentrating on your breathing and the muscles you are stretching.

4. Relax for twenty seconds. Repeat two times.

5. Repeat for the opposite leg.

Chapter 11
Cooling Down

Cooling down is every bit as important as warming up. However, it is neglected even more than warming up is. I mean, who wants to cool down after the game is already over or the recital has closed? Isn't the stretching you did prior to your workout good enough?

If you want to keep your body in a peak performance state and be ready to take on the next performance, stretching after practice is essential. As we have stated before, this is where you get the biggest gains in flexibility.

Why Is Stretching after a Workout Important?

Stretching after a workout is highly recommended, and there is science behind the reason why. When you cool down, here are some things that go on in your body:

- It helps you recover.

- Your core body temperature lowers at a slow and safe rate.

- Your blood pressure is able to decrease safely.

- The build-up of lactic acid within your muscles is allowed to release.

- The adrenaline you have accumulated is able to decrease from the "fight or flight" mode.

- This is also the time you gain the most flexibility.

- This is the most important time for static stretching.

Things to Consider When Cooling Down

- **Breathe Slower in Order to Lower Your Heart Rate**

  As you know by now, your body works harder at everything when it is in exercise mode. Your lungs, your heart, even your circulation is going over and above to provide your body with what it needs for the workout.

  During the actual time you are using the energy, like while you are dancing, this is a great setup. But, once the dance is over, your body is a bit confused. It is still desperately seeking to find a way to deliver all the extra blood and oxygen to fuel your needs but... your engine is turned off. Cooling down by slowing your breathing allows your body to change modes from a rapid heart rate to a slower, more suitable one and to do so smoothly and without chaos.

- **Your Movement Slows Down**

Gradually transition from your strenuous workout to your cool down so it will be a gentle process. You certainly don't want to send your body into shock by alarming it. If you go from full exertion to none at all, you can imagine the mixed messages your brain is sending to your muscles, organs, etc. Simply decrease your activity, little by little, by properly cooling down with a method such as static stretching.

- **Keep Hydrated**

In your cool down, be sure to drink up. Dehydration can lead to a myriad of symptoms. Adding hydration to your cool down helps to eliminate the chance of that happening. It will also refill you with energy and reduces soreness and cramping too.

- **Promotes Flexibility**

Remember the noodle. Warm muscles will stretch further. During your cool-down is the perfect time to add in some static stretches to extend your muscles and increase your flexibility. This is actual where you get most of your flexibility gains.

Cool Factors of a Cool Down Done Correctly

- Hold your poses 30-60 seconds.

- Practice gentle movements.

- Refresh your body.

- Refuel your body.

Add a Leg Stretcher to Your Cool Down

When you use your leg stretching device for slow, smooth movements, you will help your body to recover from the strain you just put it through. Your heart will have a chance to gradually decrease its heart rate and your breathing can gradually bump a notch down as well.

Add Ballet Stretch Bands in Your Cool Down

Another great way to cool down is by way of static stretching with flexibility stretch bands. This type of band will help you do passive stretches that are done without movement.

The gentle tug you will feel is subtle and optimal for cooling down.

Interesting Facts about Cooling Down

You are probably familiar with "fight or flight." It's an instinct that has been in mankind since the beginning of time when it was used to fight off tigers and to hunt food down. Your body releases adrenaline when it feels it is in trouble or needs to pump up the pace. Sometimes, it's for a basketball game. Other times, it's a false alarm and just comes out because a big bill is due and you are broke. Whatever the case, your body sends the hormone out and your vital signs react. Your blood pumps hard. Your breathing speeds up. Sweat pours. It is important to flip the switch off after your performance. That is what a cool-down does.

Cool Cool-Downs

Although you can certainly cool all your muscles down, be certain to cool down those that you used. The muscles that have elongated need to go back to their normal size. Your muscles have heated up so they physically need to cool down.

A great way to cool down is to repeat some of the movements you did during your strenuous workout but do them slower and gentler. If you ran, walk in place. If you leaped, do small, controlled leaps. You can use a stretch band or the leg stretcher too if you want.

Chapter 12
Cool-Down Exercises

Cool Roll

It's time to roll it up. Calm your body back into a relaxed state with this cool-down.

1. Stand with your arms beside your body.

2. Roll your neck with your chin to your chest.

3. Roll your back all the way down.

4. Touch your hands to the floor.

5. Roll with your back all the way back up.

6. Repeat ten times.

Roll It Up

It's time to roll it up, literally. As you begin to calm your body from its hard work back to a normally functioning zone, the same rolling exercises you used to get warmed up are perfect for cooling down as well.

1. Stand with your arms beside your body.

2. Roll your neck with your chin to your chest.

3. Roll your back all the way down, touching your hands to the floor.

4. Now, roll with your back all the way back up.

5. Repeat ten times.

Side Swipe

If you've ever gotten a cramp in your side, you will appreciate the importance of this cool-down exercise.

Remember, your circulation is greatly slowed to your digestive area during your workout, and afterward, the blood attempts to flow there again, so help it along its way with this must-do exercise.

1. Stand with your feet about a shoulder's width apart.

2. Raise your right hand above your head and reach to the side as you stretch to the left.

3. Slightly roll your back around and come back to the above stance.

4. Press down to the left to increase your side stretch.

5. Hold for ten seconds and come up to your original position.

6. Repeat ten times on the other side.

Back Thigh Stretch

Chances are, the workout or routine has placed a pretty good strain on your thighs. You have elongated them, so now it's time to get them back to their comfort zone.

1. With your feet in a wide stance, turned to the side with toe to heel, turn your body to face the side, toes pointing forward.

2. Roll forward with your back, touching your hands to the ground or if that is too intense, touch your shin instead.

3. Stretch your back and the back of your legs.

4. Hold for twenty to thirty seconds while you breathe deeply and relax the back of your thighs.

5. Return to side stance position.

6. Repeat five to ten times.

7. Repeat on the other side.

Runner's Lunge

This exercise will stretch the front of your hips.

1. Stand with your legs a shoulder's width apart, with the toes of your right foot pointing toward the heel of your left foot, like you are gearing up for a race.

2. Lunge downward.

Chapter 13

Using the Ballet Leg Stretcher and
Ballet Stretch Bands Together

A common question is, "Which works best: the leg stretcher or stretch bands?" The answer is BOTH! While they are two entirely different pieces of equipment, the effects you can achieve when using both are amazing.

What Are Stretch Bands?

Stretch bands (also called ballet stretch bands or resistance bands) are elastic-like tubes or bands that are used to help your flexibility. They come in many shapes, sizes, lengths and price ranges. Some are loop bands that resemble gigantic rubber bands and some are tube-like with handles. They are also available in different tensions with tight ones being the most difficult.

How Do Stretch Bands and a Leg Stretcher Differ?

Stretch bands work using static stretching and also from resistance. Although they serve the same purpose as that the leg stretcher does, they work completely differently. Bands are great for gradually elongating and relaxing your muscles while leg stretchers can push you beyond your normal posture by manipulating the muscle through gentle force.

How Can I Combine the Two in a Workout... and Why Should I?

Combining the use of stretch bands and a leg stretcher will give you the optimal stretch workout. It's not only effective, it also adds a little more spice to your routine. The exercises that follow will show you how to do both. Ready?

For complete instructions on how to use ballet bands see our first book, Stretching Your Limits: 30 Step-by-Step Exercises for Ballet Stretch Bands found at https://www.amazon.com/Stretching-Your-Limits-Stretches-Stretch/dp/153356177X/ in Kindle or paperback.

CONCLUSION

Exercising, like stretching, can be a lot of fun... or not. Like anything else in life, it's pretty much what you make it. Get in the groove to move with these terrific tips:

- Play your favorite music while working out. Upbeat tunes are best.

- Get a new outfit to work out in.

- Invite friends over to work out with.

- Keep a progress chart to encourage you as you bump it up a notch.

- Set goals and reward yourself for achieving them.

- Determine your workout to be fun and positive and... it will be!

Proper stretching is arguably the most important thing you can do to take your game to the next level. It enhances your strenuous workout and your performances and games too. It will also warm up your muscles so you don't get hurt, therefore helping to keep you off the bench so you can be all that you can be.

Stretching is only an asset when it is done correctly and regularly. The information and actual stretches within this book will assist you in stretching properly. Be sure to make a habit of stretching and employ it into your routine daily. It only takes one time of not stretching or not stretching properly to ruin a performance, event or game you've worked hard to prepare for.

Stretching can be enhanced by the use of a leg-stretching device that provides the ultimate in getting your body limbered up and ready for the strain you will be placing on it. It can help your muscles attain the proper resistance needed for a great warm-up, exercise and cool-down.

The stretch exercises are strategically designed to work a number of different muscles, muscle groups and joints to maximize your performance and enhance your regular routine.

Adding in another method, like ballet flexibility bands, multiplies the effects even more. With the instructions given in this book, you can mix the two types of stretching apparatuses. You now have the tools needed to take your stretching to a whole new level.

It's a long stretch to the top… but we'll help you get there.

Excerpt from...

Fruit Infused Water Recipes:

Recipes for your water bottle infuser, pitcher or jar

Chapter 2
Some Fruits Have It and Some Don't

When it comes to infusing, some fruits naturally have what it takes to send their tasty goodness and health-filled nutrients bursting into the water upon contact. Others, like bananas for instance, do not. They will turn brown and are too thick and mushy. Some simply lose their health benefits in the mix. But don't worry, we've done the homework for you. Here's a compiled list of the best fruits for infusion:

1. Tart Cherries

Tart cherries add yummy taste, loads of nutrients and many health benefits to your water. While cherries are one of the smallest fruits, they bring a pint-size package of explosive resources to the table. Be sure to use the tart (sour) variety because the sweet ones are usually best when cooked.

Enjoyed since around 70 B.C., cherries not only fill your glass full of flavor, but will keep your body in tip-top shape as well. They contain anthocyanins (flavonoids) that activate fat-burning molecules. Anthocyanins can boost your brain power, especially the cognitive functions, and lower your blood pressure.

The near-magical mini-fruits are bursting with benefits so potent, they are said to fight inflammation, infections and even cancer due to their high content of quercetin and ellagic, which can stop the spread and growth of tumors. In addition, they are rich in antioxidants, melatonin (for sleep), fiber and vitamins C and E. So there you have it. All that… and a cherry on top!

2. Cranberries

Another terrific tiny treat, cranberries provide a powerhouse of goodness. Cranberries are wildly popular in infusions for both taste and health benefits. Many love the slightly bitter twang of the berries, but if you are not a big fan, they can be mixed with other fruits, like cherries, so you can enjoy the nutritional value with only a hint of the flavor. On another note, cranberries have an acquired taste, so if you do blend them with another fruit, you might soon find that you really do like them after all.

Native to North America, the dark-colored berries were used by Native Americans for food and to color rugs long before the Pilgrims set foot on the land. They are rich in phenolic flavonoid phytochemicals, phenolic acids, fiber, manganese, copper and vitamins C, E and K. They are oozing with antioxidants that fight off free radicals. Free radicals cause illnesses, diseases, accelerated aging and a host of other problems. Notorious for battling away urinary tract infections, cranberries also help prevent cancer and boost the immune system.

CONTINUES WITH YOUR FAVORITE FRUITS....

Strawberry Mint Water

Strawberries are one of the most popular fruits for infusing. They are deliciously refreshing and are bursting with vitamins, minerals and antioxidants. Mint is a powerful pain reliever and also contains ample antioxidants, so if you want to stay healthy, this is the drink for you.

Ingredients:

- 3 cups of water

- A handful of strawberries (5-6)

- A sprig of peppermint or spearmint

Place the water in the designated compartment. Slice the strawberries and place in the fruit basket. Add the mint in with the water or in the fruit basket. Chill for several hours and enjoy.

After-Workout Infused Water Recipes

After a strenuous workout, your body needs to be replenished. Water is a must and fruits provide nutrients and minerals that are vital post-exercise as well as before. Fruits and water both help boost your energy level and help you to shed body fat while assisting in maintaining and building lean muscle. The combination also assists in increasing your metabolism. These recipes will help you to recover from all that you have put into your workout.

Watermelon Water with Rosemary

This watermelon and rosemary-infused water drink is the ideal refreshing tonic to enjoy after a workout. It is satisfying and rewarding. Watermelon contains essential vitamins and minerals and tons of water. It adds a sweet blast to the water while rosemary brings its distinguished flavor and nutrients like calcium, iron and vitamins. Rosemary is a natural pain reliever and is awesome for the circulatory system.

Ingredients:

- 3 cups of water

- 2 slices of watermelon

- 1-2 sprigs of rosemary

Slice the watermelon into small cubes. Then place the rosemary and watermelon into the fruit compartment. Add the water and drop the infuser into the water bottle. Refrigerate for at least 10 minutes before serving or longer if you wish.

Read the rest of *Fruit Infused Water Recipes* on your Kindle or in hardback at…

https://www.amazon.com/Fruit-Infused-Water-Recipes-infuser-ebook/dp/B06XV7CSF3/

Free Downloads for you

Find this book and more on amazon.com or visit our site at 14-peaks.com for free short stories and the always free book *Click and Color.*

Printed in Great Britain
by Amazon